# A Healthy Body
## from Head to Toe

Debbie Croft

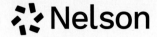

**A Healthy Body from Head to Toe**

Text: Debbie Croft
Publishers: Tania Mazzeo and Eliza Webb
Series consultant: Amanda Sutera
 Hands on Heads Consulting
Editor: Jarrah Moore
Project editor: Annabel Smith
Designer: Leigh Ashforth
Project designer: Danielle Maccarone
Illustrations: Leigh Hedstrom
Permissions researcher: Debbie Gallagher
Production controller: Renee Tome

Acknowledgements
We would like to thank the following for permission to reproduce copyright material:

Front cover: Getty Images/COROIMAGE; p. 4: Getty Images/Halfpoint Images; p. 5: iStock.com/FG Trade; p. 6: iStock.com/Nattawat Jindamaneesirikul; p. 7: iStock.com/Riska; p. 8: iStock.com/ Wavebreakmedia; p. 9: iStock.com/andreswd; p. 10: iStock.com/ vitapix; p. 11 (top): Shutterstock.com/Yavdat, (bottom): iStock.com/ Charday Penn; iStock.com/georgeclerk; p. 13 (top): Getty Images/ Jonathan Kirn, (bottom): Shutterstock.com/Natallia Yaumenenka; p. 14: iStock.com/youngvet; p. 15: Shutterstock.com/Dejan Dundjerski; p. 16: iStock.com/JuiceBros; p. 18: iStock.com/InkkStudios; p. 19: iStock.com/ Drazen Zigic; p. 20: Getty Images/Westend61; p. 21 (top): iStock.com/ Giselleflissak, (bottom): Shutterstock.com/Master1305; p. 22: Getty Images/Peter Cade; p. 23: Alamy Stock Photo/Erickson Stock.

Every effort has been made to trace and acknowledge copyright. However, if any infringement has occurred, the publishers tender their apologies and invite the copyright holders to contact them.

NovaStar

Text © 2024 Cengage Learning Australia Pty Limited
Illustrations © 2024 Cengage Learning Australia Pty Limited

ISBN 978 0 17 033405 1

**Cengage Learning Australia**
Level 5, 80 Dorcas Street
Southbank VIC 3006 Australia
Phone: 1300 790 853
Email: aust.nelsonprimary@cengage.com

For learning solutions, visit **cengage.com.au**

Printed in China by 1010 Printing International Ltd
1 2 3 4 5 6 7 28 27 26 25 24

*Nelson acknowledges the Traditional Owners and Custodians of the lands of all First Nations Peoples. We pay respect to Elders past and present, and extend that respect to all First Nations Peoples today.*

# Contents

# What Is a Healthy Body?

When your body is healthy, you feel well. You have lots of energy, too.

Eating healthy foods and staying active help you feel well most of the time. Getting enough sleep each night helps, too.

When your body is healthy, you can get out and have fun.

Getting enough sleep helps your body to stay healthy.

But sometimes, things can go wrong with parts of your body, and you can get hurt or feel unwell. Let's find out about the human body and how to keep it healthy – from head to toe!

## Your Beating Heart

Your heart beats about 80 times each minute. That's more than 100 000 times each day!

# Your Head

We'll start right at the very top of your body – your head!

Sometimes you can get a pain inside your head. This is known as a headache, and it can feel like someone is beating a drum in there! If you have a headache, you usually don't want to play or be active.

Doing schoolwork can be hard when you have a headache.

Drinking lots of water helps keep headaches away.

A headache can be caused by not having enough water in your body, or by missing meals. Drinking plenty of water and eating lots of healthy food each day can stop you getting a headache.

Resting in a quiet place, away from bright light, can help make you feel better when you have a headache.

# Your Nose

If you bump your nose, or blow it too hard, it can start to bleed. But try not to worry too much!

Inside your nose are tiny **blood vessels**. They can tear very easily, but they **repair** themselves quickly, too. If your nose starts to bleed, sit down and lean forward a little. Use a tissue to squeeze the soft front parts of your nose together. It will usually stop bleeding after a few minutes.

It's important to lean forward when your nose is bleeding.

## Your Own Air Filter

Your nose does a really important job! It cleans, warms and dries the air you breathe before the air goes to your lungs.

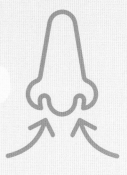

Your nose helps you breathe clean, warm air.

# Your Throat

Now, open wide – let's look down your throat!

Your throat is the front part of your neck that takes food to your stomach, and air to your lungs.

You might get a sore throat, a cold or the flu if a **germ** gets into your body. This germ can make your throat red and sore for a few days.

A sore throat can be very uncomfortable.

There are lots of ways to treat a sore throat. You could try drinking warm water with honey and lemon juice, or **gargling** some warm, salty water.

Warm drinks can make a sore throat feel better.

# Germs, Germs, Go Away!

To help stop the spread of germs:

- wash your hands with soap and water
- use your arm to cover your nose and mouth when you cough or sneeze
- don't share drinks and food
- stay at home if you are unwell.

# Your Arms and Hands

Have you ever broken a bone in your body?

You can break a bone in your arm or your wrist, or you can break one of the many small bones in your hands and fingers.

If you fall over, or fall off your bike or skateboard, you could break a bone. Then you might need to have a **cast** on the injured body part.

This modern cast can protect your hand and wrist while the bone mends.

A cast stops the broken bone from moving, so it can heal.
Most breaks mend in a few weeks.

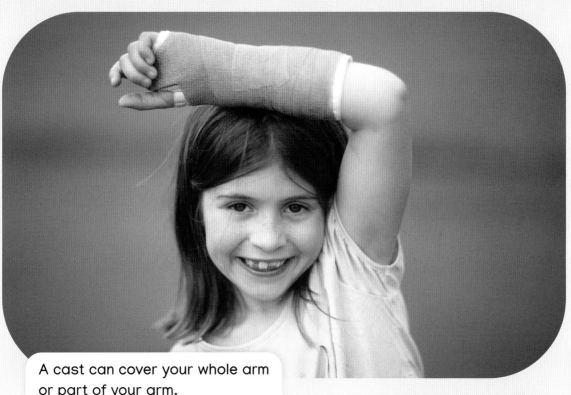

A cast can cover your whole arm
or part of your arm.

## So Many Bones

Starting at your shoulder,
and moving down to the tips
of your fingers, you have a
total of 32 bones in each arm.

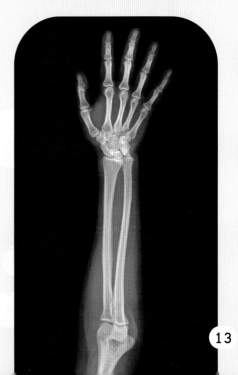

# Your Torso

Now, let's talk about your torso. The torso is all of your body, except your head, arms and legs.

Your lungs are in the top part of your torso. If you have asthma, it affects your lungs and can make it harder for you to breathe. Dust, **pollen** from grass or trees, or exercise can make asthma worse.

Pollen can make you sneeze and it can make asthma worse.

You can use an inhaler (also called a "puffer") to breathe in medicine to help your lungs work better.

An inhaler lets you breathe in medicine for asthma.

**Did You Know?**

You can't breathe and swallow at the same time.

Your **gut** starts at your mouth and goes all the way down through your torso. Food goes into your gut when you eat and leaves your body as **waste**.

When you don't look after your gut, you can feel tired, and your stomach can feel sore or uncomfortable.

Most of the goodness you get from the food you eat is **absorbed** in the gut. Eating lots of fresh fruit, vegetables and grains helps to keep your gut healthy. Drinking plenty of water is very important, too.

Eating lots of fresh food keeps your gut healthy.

# Your Gut

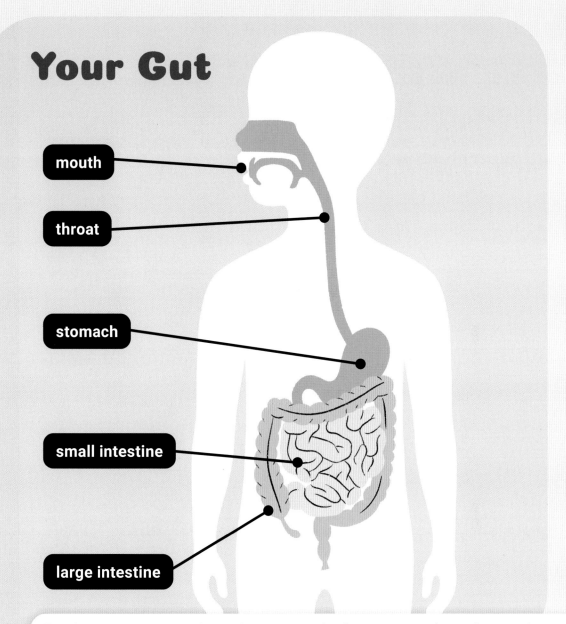

mouth

throat

stomach

small intestine

large intestine

Food enters your gut through your mouth, then passes through your throat, stomach, and small and large intestines before leaving your body.

## Passing Through

It usually takes between one and three days for food to pass all the way through your gut.

# Your Legs and Feet

Your legs are joined to the bottom of your torso. And at the ends of your legs are your feet.

If you trip or fall, you can **sprain** your knee or ankle. This happens if your foot or knee twists or rolls suddenly. You may need to wrap the sprained body part in a tight bandage and rest it for a few days.

Wrapping a sprained ankle with a bandage will protect it while it's healing.

It's important to warm up your legs before you start playing a sport or moving quickly. A good warm-up slowly stretches your muscles so they can safely do bigger, faster movements.

Stretch your legs before playing a sport so you don't pull a muscle.

## Muscles and Bones

Your body has more than 600 muscles and 206 bones. A quarter of the bones in your body are in your feet!

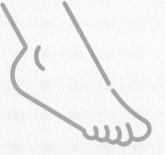

# Your Skin

Finally, let's look at your skin – it covers your whole body from head to toe.

Some types of skin burn easily in the sun. To take care of your skin, you can:

- wear a hat, t-shirt and sunglasses
- use SPF 50+ sunscreen
- stay in the shade when you can.

With a hat, sunscreen and sunglasses, your skin and eyes are protected.

Make sure you spread sunscreen over all of your bare skin when playing in the sun.

## Thick and Thin

The thickest skin on your body is on your feet, and the thinnest skin is on your eyelids!

# Staying Healthy

You feel well when your body is healthy. Drinking plenty of water, eating well and staying active will help keep you healthy.

Learning about your body and things you can do if something goes wrong will help, too.

Eating healthy food helps keep your body healthy.

By staying healthy from head to toe, you'll be able to play with your friends and have lots of fun!

# Glossary

| | |
|---|---|
| **absorbed** (*verb*) | taken in or soaked up |
| **blood vessels** (*noun*) | tiny tubes that blood flows through |
| **cast** (*noun*) | a hard shell put around a body part to keep it from moving |
| **gargling** (*verb*) | moving liquid around your mouth and throat before spitting it out |
| **germ** (*noun*) | a tiny living thing that can cause disease |
| **gut** (*noun*) | a number of long tubes that food travels through in your body |
| **pollen** (*noun*) | powder from some plants that travels on the wind |
| **repair** (*verb*) | to fix something that is broken |
| **sprain** (*verb*) | to twist and damage the join between two bones |
| **waste** (*noun*) | things that the body gets rid of |

# Index